PICTURE GUIDE
TO HISTORIC
PLYMOUTH

Edited by ROSE T. BRIGGS

Published by the Pilgrim Society
1963

"As one candle may light a thousand, so the light here kindled has shown ... in some sort to our whole nation."   *Bradford*

ISBN #0-940628-05-8

Copyright by the Pilgrim Society 1963

7TH PRINTING 1983

CONTENTS

Antiquarian House 35
Brewster Park and its Memorials 16
Brewster Spring 17
Burial Hill: the Fort; the Graves; the Guns 22
Church of the Pilgrimage 19
Coles Hill 14
Combination Tickets 39
First House and 1627 House 12
First Parish, Plymouth 19
First Street (Leyden Street) 16
Forefathers' Monument 25
Harlow Old Fort House 32
Howland House 31
Map: Guide to Plymouth and its History 20-21
Massasoit (statue) 15
Mayflower II (ship) 11
Mayflower Passengers 7
Mayflower Society House 34
Memorial Hall 36
Old Colony Memorial (newspaper) 37
Pilgrim Hall, Museum of Pilgrim Treasures 26
Pilgrim Maiden (statue) 17
Pilgrim Mother (statue) 13
Pilgrim Progress 18
Pilgrim Story 5
Plimoth Plantation 29
Plymouth Area Chamber of Commerce 38
Plymouth Colony Records 36
Plymouth County Court House and Registry of Deeds 36
Plymouth Rock 8
Public Library 37
Sarcophagus 14
Sparrow House 30
Spooner House 33
Tourist Information 38
Town Offices 36
Town Records 36
Wharves 37

DEPARTURE FROM HOLLAND *Pilgrim Hall*
"But the tide which stays for no man calling them away . . . their reverend Pastor . . . commended them to the Lord and His blessing." *Bradford*

THANKSGIVING *Pilgrim Hall*
"And so instead of famine God gave them plenty." *Bradford*

THE PILGRIM STORY

"They knew that they were Pilgrims..."
Bradford

In the reign of King James, a group of men and women, living near the village of Scrooby in the north of England, left the English Church, and "as the Lord's free people, joined themselves... to walk in all His ways, known or to be made known to them, whatever it should cost them." This exposed them to serious legal penalties, and soon drove them to Holland, "where they heard there was freedom of religion for all men." They settled in Leyden; but after about twelve years, they decided to seek "some of those vast unpeopled parts of America which were fruitful and fit for habitation."

A group of London merchants were persuaded to back the venture. The Pilgrims, with little money to invest, were obliged to contribute their labor. At the end of seven years, the assets of the colony were to be divided between the merchants and the settlers; until then, all labor and assets were to be part of the "Common Stock" of the colony.

A "Patent," authorizing the settlement, was procured from the Virginia Company, which had already begun its colony at Jamestown; a ship, the MAYFLOWER, was hired; more colonists, some recruited by the London merchants, were added to the Leyden group. After many difficulties, they finally left Plymouth, England, September 16, 1620. The voyage was stormy, and when land was sighted, it proved to be Cape Cod, outside the jurisdiction of the Virginia Company. As their Patent was therefore useless, the COMPACT, a signed agreement to obey the officers and laws they should set up for themselves, was improvised as a basis of government. The original document has disappeared; the wording is preserved in the first report of the colony, printed in London in 1622. This is among the Pilgrim treasures in Pilgrim Hall.

After a month of exploration, while the MAYFLOWER lay anchored in what is now Provincetown Harbor, a party of Pilgrims and sailors landed at Plymouth, December 21, 1620, and found it "a place very good for situation." The ship, with the rest of the colonists, was brought to Plymouth, and the work of settlement began.

All winter the work of building and unloading went on, impeded by bad weather, and an epidemic which reduced the colony by half. At one time there were but six or seven persons well enough to nurse the rest. Early in April, the MAYFLOWER sailed back to England, leaving the Pilgrims to survive if they could.

All winter they were conscious of Indians, but could not make contact with them. In March, a single Indian appeared, and greeted them in English. He soon brought another, called Squanto, who had actually been in England. This man was the only survivor of a tribe which had once lived at Plymouth, but had succumbed to an epidemic which decimated the Indians from Maine to Rhode Island. Squanto remained at Plymouth, and was of great service to the Colony. They were also visited by Massasoit, the principal chief of the region. The treaty they made with him was advantageous to both sides, and faithfully kept as long as its makers lived.

The summer passed in planting and cultivating their fields, fishing, trading, and preparing a cargo for the next ship. Then "they began to gather in their harvest, and to fit up their houses for the winter, being well recovered in health and strength, and having all things in good plenty." "Their harvest being gotten in," writes Edward Winslow, "the Governor sent four men fowling, so they might in a special manner rejoice together after they had gathered the fruit of their labor." Many of the Indians came to the festivities, "among the rest Massasoit and ninety of his men, whom for three days they entertained and feasted."

Plymouth Colony proved that permanent settlement in New England was possible, if homes for settlers, rather than dividends for investors, was the object. The colony lasted as an independent unit for about seventy years. In 1692 it became part of-the Colony of Massachusetts Bay. Plymouth, the first settlement, has been inhabited continuously since the landing in 1620.

THE MAYFLOWER PASSENGERS from Bradford's History

"The names of those that came first in the year 1620 and were . . . the first beginners of all the colonies in New England. . ."

*MR. JOHN CARVER (governor)
*Katherine, his wife
Desire Minter and a maid
John Howland; Roger Wilder
Wm. Latham; *Jasper More
MR. WM. BREWSTER; wife Mary
Love; Wrestling (sons)
Richard More and *his brother
MR. EDWARD WINSLOW
*Elizabeth, his wife; *Ellen More
George Soule; *Elias Storey
WM. BRADFORD; *wife Dorothy
MR. ISAAC ALLERTON; *wife Mary
Bartholomew; Remember; Mary
*John Hooke
MR. SAMUEL FULLER (physician)
*William Button (died at sea)
*JOHN CRACKSTON; son John
CAPT. MYLES STANDISH; *wife Rose
*MR. CHRISTOPHER MARTIN; *wife
*Solomon Prower; *John Langmore
*MR. WM. MULLINS and *his wife
*Joseph; Priscilla
*Robert Carter
*MR. WM. WHITE; wife Susanna
Resolved; Peregrine (sons)
(Peregrine was born on the MAYFLOWER in Provincetown harbor)
*Wm. Holbeck; *Edw. Thompson
MR. STEPHEN HOPKINS
Elizabeth, his wife
Giles; Constance; Damaris
Oceanus (born at sea)
Edw. Doty; Edw. Lister
MR. RICHARD WARREN

JOHN BILLINGTON
Ellen, his wife
John; Francis
*EDW. TILLEY, *wife Ann
Henry Sampson; Humility Cooper
*JOHN TILLEY; *his wife
Elizabeth Tilley
FRANCIS COOKE; son John
*THOMAS ROGERS
Joseph, his son
*THOMAS TINKER
*wife; *son
*JOHN RIGDALE
*wife Alice
*JAMES CHILTON; *wife
Mary Chilton
*EDW. FULLER; *wife
Samuel, their son
*JOHN TURNER; two sons
FRANCIS EATON
*Sarah, his wife
Samuel, infant son
*MOSES FLETCHER
*JOHN GOODMAN
*THOMAS WILLIAMS
*DEGORY PRIEST
*EDMOND MARGESON
PETER BROWN
*RICHARD BRITTERIDGE
*RICHARD CLARKE
RICHARD GARDINER
GILBERT WINSLOW
JOHN ALDEN
*JOHN ALLERTON
*THOMAS ENGLISH
*WM. TREVOR, seaman
. . . ELY, seaman

*died first year

PLYMOUTH ROCK — Plymouth Rock was identified as the landing-place of the Pilgrims by Thomas Faunce, last Ruling Elder of the Plymouth Church; he had the information from his father, who came to Plymouth in the ship ANNE, 1623. Several members of the MAYFLOWER'S landing-party were still living in Elder Faunce's boyhood. On the eve of the Revolution, the part of the Rock now visible was carried to Town Square and placed at the foot of the Liberty Pole. On July 4, 1834, it was carried in procession to Pilgrim Hall to join the Pilgrim treasures preserved there.

In the middle of the last century, the Pilgrim Society acquired that part of the Rock which the patriots of 1774 had found impossible to move from its original bed. A granite canopy, dedicated in 1867, was erected over it. In 1880, the upper part of the Rock was united with the base.

At the time of the 300th Anniversary of the Landing, the old wharves, no longer needed, were removed, the area was re-landscaped, and the Rock restored to tide-level, where the winter storms still break over it as they did in Pilgrim days. The area became a State Park, and the guardianship of the Rock was transferred from the Pilgrim Society to the Commonwealth of Massachusetts.

The present portico was dedicated November 29, 1921. It was designed by McKim, Mead, and White, and is the gift of the National Society of the Colonial Dames of America.

"*Here is a stone which the feet of a few outcasts press for an instant, and the stone becomes famous; it is treasured by a great people; its very dust is shared as a relic.*" *DeTocqueville — 1834*

MAYFLOWER II   Mayflower II is a full-scale replica of the vessel which brought the Pilgrims to Plymouth in 1620.

Built in England from plans developed for Plimoth Plantation by Naval Architect William A. Baker, she was sailed across the Atlantic in 1957.

Now wholly owned and operated by Plimoth Plantation, a non-profit educational foundation, the vessel is berthed at State Pier on the waterfront from mid-April through Thanksgiving Week.

Exhibits aboard ship are designed to show how the ship was operated and how the crew and passengers lived aboard during the 1620 crossing. Costumed guides and hostesses are on hand to answer visitors' questions.

Little technical information is known about the Pilgrims' Mayflower. The only certain knowledge of her is contained in Governor Bradford's account of her voyage to the New World in which he stated she was of 180 tons burden, and gives an indication of her rig.

Taking what was known about the Mayflower and incorporating it into his design, Baker produced a typical English merchantman of the 17th century. In arriving at an approximation of the original vessel's dimensions, he studied ships of the period and used the tonnage computation rules of the day.

The Mayflower II is a ship of 181 tons burden. She is 104 feet long overall with a 78 ft. 8 in. waterline, a beam of 25½ feet and a draft of 13 feet.

She is square rigged on her fore and main masts with a lateen sail on her mizzen mast. Her cordage is of Italian hemp; her sails are linen and were cut and sewed by hand.

Tied up alongside Mayflower II is a shallop, a full-scale replica of the open sailing and rowing workboat used by the Pilgrims. When the Mayflower anchored off Provincetown, the shallop was used in the explorations that finally brought the Pilgrims to Plymouth. Later it served in their fishing and trading voyages.

The shallop was built in Plymouth, and like the Mayflower, was designed by William A. Baker.

First House and 1627 House are on the Waterfront near Plymouth Rock.

Repairing A Thatched Roof at Plimoth Plantation.

THE PILGRIM MOTHER

On the water-front, near Plymouth Rock, there stands, in a landscaped enclosure, the granite figure of a Pilgrim woman, which has come to be known as "The Pilgrim Mother." Behind her, a tall granite shaft supports a fountain which overflows into a quiet pool at her feet. Cool stone benches invite the tourist to rest and reflection.

This memorial is the gift of the National Society, Daughters of the American Revolution, in memory of the heroic women of the MAYFLOWER. It was designed by McKim, Mead, and White; the sculptor was Paul O. Jennewein.

On the shaft of the fountain are the names of the women who came in the MAYFLOWER, and the inscription:

> *"They brought up their families in sturdy virtue and a living faith in God without which nations perish."*

MEMORIAL FOUNTAIN
TO THE WOMEN OF
THE MAYFLOWER

COLES HILL
SARCOPHAGUS
STATUE OF
MASSASOIT

Behind Plymouth Rock rises a steep grassy hill, called Coles Hill from James Cole, who held land there in 1633. The view over the harbor is superb.

Here, in an abandoned cornfield, whose Indian owners had perished not long before in a mysterious epidemic, the Pilgrims buried those who died in the "general sickness" of the first winter. The list amounts to half their number. Some families were wiped out completely. Their deaths were part of the price of founding the colony, but they are often forgotten, for they have no further history, and no descendants to honor their memory. Their names are inscribed on the seaward side of a granite sarcophagus erected here in their honor; on the opposite side is written:

> "In weariness and painfulness, in hunger and cold, they laid the foundations of a state wherein every man ... should have liberty to worship God in his own way."

The sarcophagus holds the bones which have been discovered at various times in this first burying ground. It was given by the General Society of Mayflower Descendants, and was dedicated September 8, 1921.

STATUE OF MASSASOIT Near the Sarcophagus stands a heroic bronze statue in honor of Massasoit, chief of the Wampanoag Indians, whose friendship was an important factor in the peaceful development of the Pilgrim colony. The statue is by Cyrus Dallin; it was erected in 1921 by the Improved Order of Red Men.

Other memorials include two stone seats, one presented by the Pennsylvania Society of New England Women, the other by the Society of Daughters of Colonial Wars, Commonwealth of Massachusetts.

In 1961, Coles Hill was designated by the National Park Service a registered National Historic Landmark. This is recorded on a bronze tablet near the head of the steps leading up from the Rock. The area is owned and maintained by the Pilgrim Society.

THE FIRST STREET
(Leyden St.)
TOWN BROOK
BREWSTER PARK

Site of the Common House

The first concern of the Pilgrims was to provide shelter on shore for themselves and their goods. On January 6, 1621, they laid out their street, parallel to the Town Brook. They divided themselves into nineteen households, and assigned to each a garden plot fronting on "the Street."

A "Common House" for the general use of the Colony was the first to be built. It sheltered the men working on shore and their supplies as they were unloaded. It served as a hospital for the sick. Here, until the fort was built in 1622, the community assembled for worship and for public business. The Commonwealth of Massachusetts has marked the site with a tablet recording that here the right of popular suffrage was exercised on February 21, 1621, when Myles Standish was chosen Captain by majority vote.

Seven houses and four buildings "for the use of the plantation" were built the first year. In 1627, Isaac De Rasieres, Secretary of the Dutch colony of the New Amsterdam, visiting Plymouth, describes it as a thriving settlement of planked houses, neatly impaled, and guarded by a fort on the hill, which also served as a meeting place for worship and for public business. It is this settlement which Plimoth Plantation reproduces in its Pilgrim Village.

For many years "the Street" needed no other name. Since 1834 it has been called Leyden Street, in honor of the Dutch city which had sheltered the Pilgrims.

On the south side of the first street, "the garden plottes of those which came first, layed out 1620" ran down to the Town Brook. Here herring were caught in April to fertilize the corn fields, and many springs supplied the households of the town. Elder Brewster's spring is still flowing. It has been piped up from brook level to where his house stood, on the site now occupied by the Post Office. Below, Brewster Park follows the Brook on both sides to its mouth.

Brewster Park, which is under the care of the Park Department of the Town of Plymouth, was projected by the Town at the instigation of the Plymouth Woman's Club; some of the first planting was given by Mrs. William H. Forbes, daughter of Ralph Waldo Emerson and his wife, Lydian Jackson of Plymouth. At the foot of the steps leading down into the garden is a tablet in memory of Mrs. Emerson and her brother, Dr. Charles T. Jackson, whose experimental work with ether as an anesthetic paved the way for its successful use. In 1923, the Daughters of the American Colonists gave a memorial bench in remembrance of those daughters of American Colonists who came to Plymouth in the ship, ANNE, 1623. At the edge of a pool stands a bronze statue of a young Pilgrim woman by H. H. Kitson presented to the Town by the National Society of New England Women. It is inscribed:

"To those intrepid English women whose courage, fortitude, and devotion brought a new nation into being, this statue of the Pilgrim Maiden is dedicated."

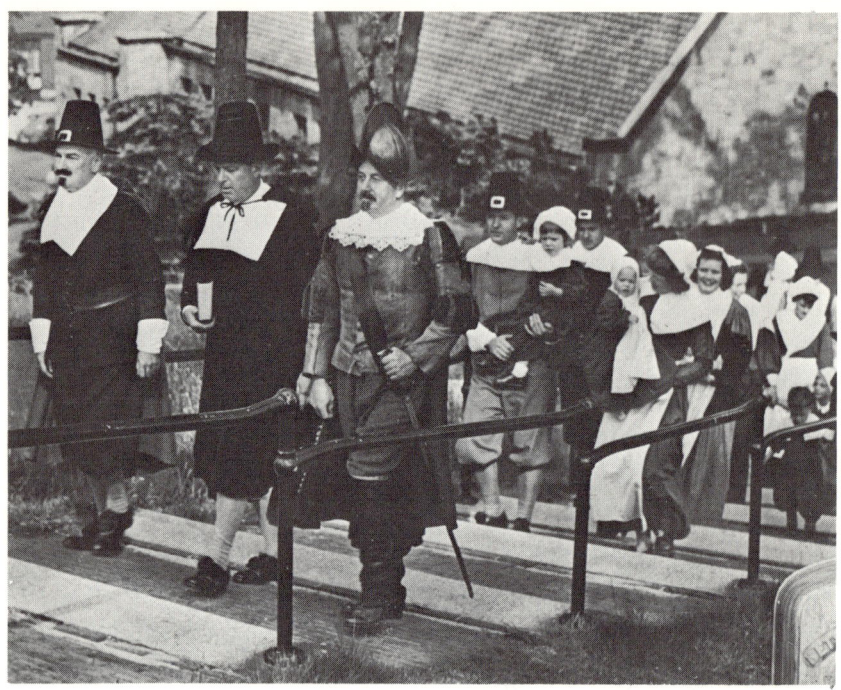

THE PILGRIM PROGRESS, instituted by the Town of Plymouth in 1921, takes place every Friday in August at five o'clock, and on Thanksgiving Day. Each marcher represents one of the Pilgrims, — man, woman, or child — who survived the first winter. A list of the Pilgrim households, noting who lived and who died, is given in Bradford's history. The list is carefully followed. The Pilgrims assemble at beat of drum on the brow of Coles Hill, and march to meeting under arms, as described by Isaac De Rasieres in his eye-witness account. They march up the First Street to the site of the Fort-meeting house on Burial Hill, where a short service is held. The psalms sung are those used by the Pilgrims in Holland and in Plymouth; the passages read are from Pilgrim sources. Thus the present citizens of Plymouth faithfully re-live the Sabbath procession of the Pilgrims to worship.

FIRST PARISH CHURCH
CHURCH OF THE PILGRIMAGE

At the head of Town Square stands the fifth meeting house of the First Parish, Plymouth. A tablet bears this inscription:

> *"The Church of Scrooby, Leyden, and the Mayflower, gathered on this hillside in 1620, has preserved unbroken records and maintained a continuous ministry, its first covenant being still the basis of its fellowship . . ."*

The present building, the doorway of which was inspired by that of the church in England where Gov. Bradford was christened, was erected in 1898. From this church were founded:

First Church, Duxbury 1632   First Church, Plympton 1698
"   "   Marshfield 1632   "   "   Kingston 1717
"   "   Eastham 1646   Second "   Plymouth 1738
Third Church, Plymouth 1801 (Church of the Pilgrimage)

At the beginning of the 19th century, many New England churches, among them the First Parish of Plymouth, became identified with the movement from which the Unitarian Universalist denomination developed. In 1801, part of the membership of the First Parish, "adhering to the belief of the Fathers, and on the basis of the original creed," withdrew to organize the Third Church, which in 1840 took the name of Church of the Pilgrimage. Its meeting house, built in 1840, stands on the north side of Town Square.

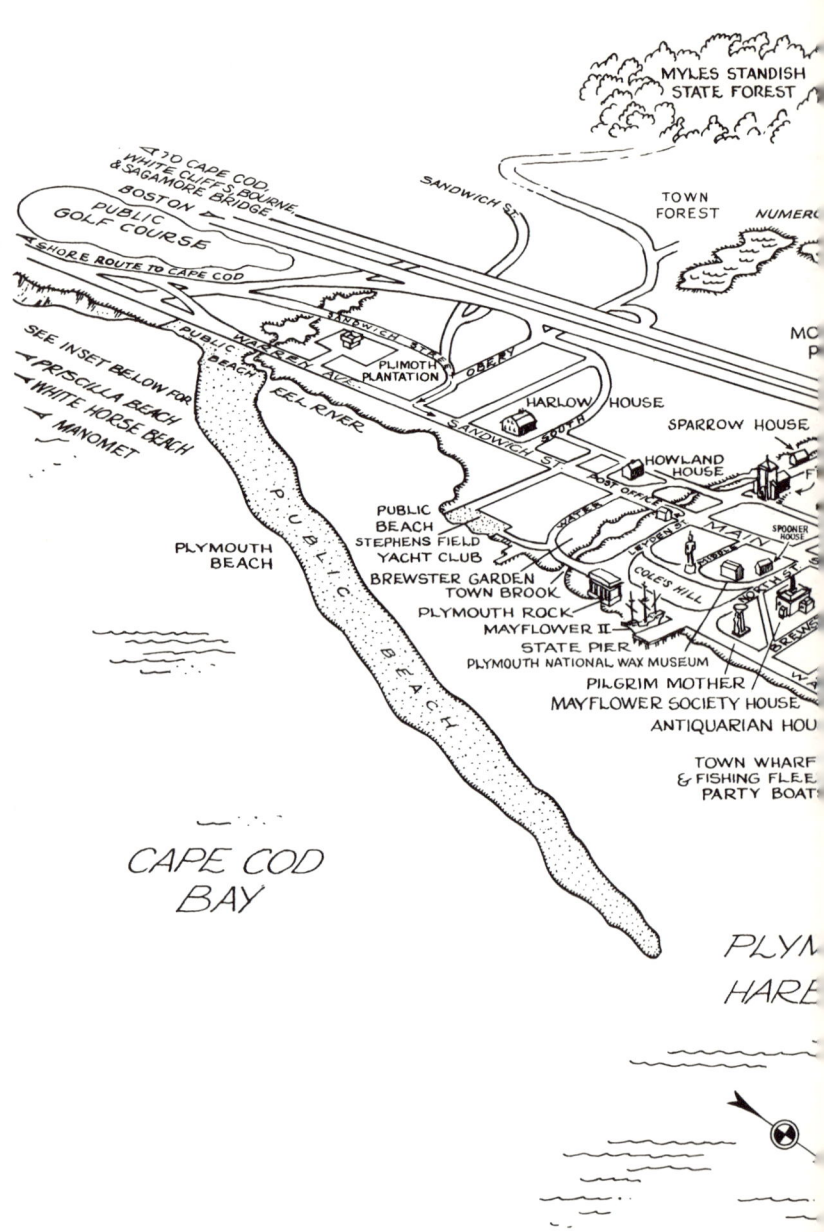

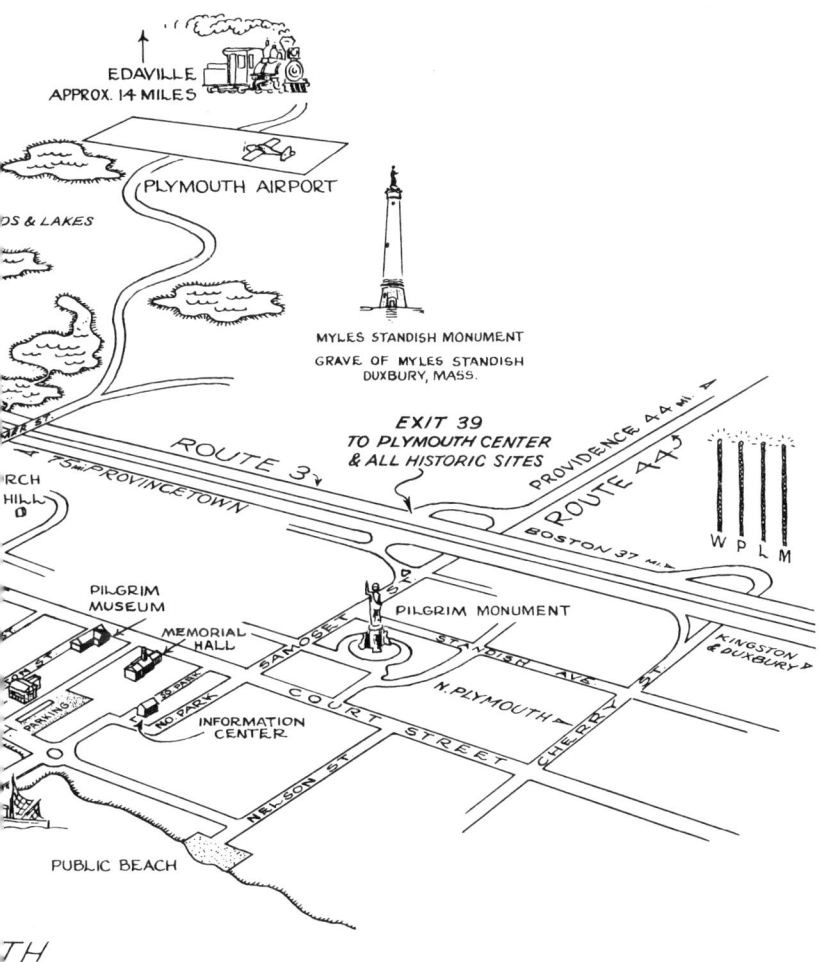

A GUIDE TO
PLYMOUTH
And Its History

BURIAL HILL:
THE FORT-MEETING HOUSE

"Upon a hill they have a large square house with a flat roof, made of thick sawn planks, stayed with oak beams, on the top of which are six cannon, which ... command the surrounding country. The lower part they use for their church, where they preach Sundays and the usual holidays."

So De Rasieres describes the Pilgrims' Fort-meeting house. It was part of a careful system of fortification, begun in 1621 when Capt. Jones helped the Pilgrims unload and mount four small cannon from the MAYFLOWER. In 1622, warned by the massacre at Jamestown, they built their Fort, and surrounded the town with a strong stockade which was guarded night and day. The Fort was repaired in 1633, 1635, 1642; in 1643 a watchtower was built near by. After King Philip's War, when danger from the Indians was over, the Fort was dismantled. In 1876 a marble tablet was erected to mark the site, and here the Pilgrim Progess holds its service.

"With arms in their hands they gathered to worship God. But they were armed ... not that they might prevail by force, but that they might do right though they perished."   *Calvin Coolidge — 1920*

BURIAL HILL: Near the site of the Fort-meeting house
THE GUNS   stand two ancient cannon; they were presented to Plymouth October 4, 1921, by the British government, through the good offices of the Honorable Artillery Company of London (1537) and the Ancient and Honorable Artillery Company of Massachusetts (1638). These guns are the same age and type as those mounted on this spot in 1622. One is a "Minion," cast in 1557; the other a "Sackeret," cast in 1550. The first account of the colony mentions such guns:

"March 3, 1621   The master [Capt. Jones of the MAYFLOWER] came on shore with many of his Sailors, and brought with him one of the great pieces, called a minion, and helped us to draw it up the hill, with another piece that lay on the shore, and mounted them, and a sacker [sackeret] and two bases [very small cannon]."

                                      Mourt's Relation   1622

BURIAL HILL: THE GRAVES

When "Fort Hill" became "Burial Hill" is not recorded. The earliest graves were unmarked, and many of the "first commers" are buried in later settlements, where they followed their sons or established themselves as pioneers from Plymouth. Governor Bradford is thought to be buried near his son, Major William Bradford, on the brow of the hill overlooking the harbor. A monument marks the spot, with a Latin inscription signifying:

"What your fathers attained with such difficulty, Do not basely relinquish."

Pilgrim John Howland's grave is on the westerly slope of the hill. He died in 1673, being over 80; "the last man that was left of those that came over in the Shipp called the Mayflower that lived in Plymouth." Near his grave is that of Edward Gray. This headstone (1681) is the earliest of the six 17th-century stones on the hill.

Near the site of the Fort-meeting house, is a monument to the Cushman family. Robert Cushman, a member of the Leyden congregation, was the Pilgrims' chief agent in London. He visited Plymouth in 1621, leaving his son Thomas, who grew up to succeed Brewster as Elder of the Plymouth church. Elder Cushman married Mary Allerton. She died in 1699, the last of the MAYFLOWER passengers.

Other interesting stones commemorate Dr. Francis LeBaron (1704), and Adoniram Judson (1850), Baptist missionary to Burma. On the site of the school where he taught, a bronze tablet honors Alexander Scammell, who left his desk in the Plymouth Grammar School to serve in the Revolution, and was killed at Yorktown. Many stones are notable for their quaint carving and inscriptions, especially a group on the brow of the hill, just north of the steps leading up from the Town Square.

FOREFATHERS' MONUMENT

On the summit of a hill behind the Town, stands the National Monument to the Forefathers. A heroic figure of Faith, pointing to heaven, surmounts a massive granite pedestal. Below are seated Liberty, peace flourishing under her protection and tyranny overthrown by her power; Law attended by justice and mercy; Education, with wisdom on one side and youth led by experience on the other; and Morality, between a prophet and an evangelist holding the Commandments in her left hand and the scroll of Revelation in her right. Below the seated figures, four marble bas-reliefs recall significant episodes in Pilgrim history: the departure from Holland, the signing of the Compact, the landing at Plymouth, and the treaty with Massasoit. The monument is 81 feet high, the pedestal measuring 45 feet and the figure of Faith 36.

"To procure... a suitable lot... for the erection of a monument to perpetuate the memory of the virtues, the enterprise, and the unparalleled sufferings of their ancestors" was a primary purpose of the Pilgrim Society, as expressed in its charter. Contributions came from the Federal Government, from the Commonwealth of Massachusetts and the State of Connecticut, and from 11000 individuals throughout the country. The cost was $150,000. The design was by Hammatt Billings. The cornerstone was laid August 1, 1859; the monument was dedicated August 1, 1889.

The National Monument to the Forefathers is maintained by the Pilgrim Society.

PILGRIM HALL MUSEUM OF PILGRIM TREASURES
1824

Driving south through Plymouth on Route 3A, the traveler cannot fail to notice Pilgrim Hall on his left, a porticoed granite building in the Greek Revival or "temple" style.

Here are housed many personal possessions of the MAYFLOWER passengers and their descendants, — furniture, household utensils, clothing, the books they read and wrote. Examination of these Pilgrim treasures offers a unique opportunity to visualize what the Pilgrims were like, and how they lived.

The Pilgrim Society, which maintains Pilgrim Hall, Coles Hill, and the Forefathers' Monument, was founded in 1820 to insure appreciation of the Pilgrim contribution to the American heritage. Pilgrim Hall, built in 1824, was designed by Alexander Parris, architect of St. Paul's, Boston, and has been in continuous use ever since. It is one of the oldest museum buildings in America. Although the Hall has undergone several changes, fireproofing in 1880, addition of the library wing in 1904, and substitution of the granite portico for the original wooden one in 1922, its essential appearance has not been altered.

In the Main Gallery may be seen the "great chairs" of Governor Carver and Elder Brewster, names as important to collectors of furniture as to historians. Here also are the chairs of Governor Bradford and Governor Winslow; Myles Standish's swords and razors; the cradle of Peregrine White, born on the MAYFLOWER in Provincetown harbor; some of the books printed in Leyden by Elder Brewster; and a portrait of Edward Winslow, the only known likeness of a Pilgrim. In the Lower Gallery are shown 17th and 18th-century household equipment and Indian artifacts. The Ship Room contains the skeleton of the SPARROWHAWK, the only example which remains of the ships which explored and colonized New England. Bound for Virginia in 1627, she went aground on Cape Cod, was buried in the sand, and came to light again in 1863. Pilgrim Hall Library, open to the public as well as to scholars and genealogists, contains many out-of-print works on Plymouth and New England history, and some rare 17th and 18th-century volumes.

In recent years the Pilgrim Society has expanded its policy to include preservation of information, documents, and artifacts relating to later Plymouth history. From time to time, "Notes" are published, based on research done by members of the Society. Every effort is made by this fine old organization to interpret the Pilgrim story and Plymouth history vividly and intelligently, following the best museum practice. Thus the purpose for which the Society was founded in the nineteenth century is continued in the twentieth.

Harvest Scene at Plimoth Plantation.

Interior Scene at Plimoth Plantation.

PLIMOTH
PLANTATION
1627

Plimoth Plantation, located at Eel River on Route 3A is a re-creation of the original Pilgrim Colony as it looked in 1627, some seven years after the Pilgrims landed at Plymouth Rock.

Historical and archaeological research have gone into the planning of this replica village to make it as much like the original as possible. Although the site of the original village is now the business center of Plymouth, the topography of the present Plantation is almost identical with that of the original.

On a hill overlooking the village and commanding the approaches from the sea is the Fort-Meetinghouse with cannons poking through the ports of the gun deck. Atop the fort near the cannons, a scarlet-cloaked "Myles Standish" demonstrates for visitors the loading and firing of a matchlock musket. In the large room below, a typical Pilgrim religious service is represented by life-like mannequins.

Halfway down the hill to seaward is a village surrounded on three sides by a palisade of pointed logs. Both sides of the village are lined with vertically planked or clapboarded houses with thatched or wooden shake roofs, and oiled paper windows. Huge stone fireplaces take up one whole wall of the tiny houses and are used for cooking and as the source of heat.

It's a functioning village in which costumed guides and hostess move about, busy at tasks of the period. Some demonstrations are as simple as cooking a stew over an open fireplace; others involve more demanding skills such as cloth dyeing, shake splitting or nail making.

The re-created Plantation has been built by a non-profit educational foundation which also owns and exhibits Mayflower II, two replica Pilgrim Houses near Plymouth Rock, and a replica of a small Pilgrim sailing craft called a shallop.

SPARROW HOUSE The Richard Sparrow House, Summer Street, was built about 1640. It probably is the oldest house now standing in Plymouth. A fine example of 17th-century building, it shows clearly how it was enlarged, a few years after it was built, from a house which had a single room on the ground floor, with a single chamber over it, to the "salt box" type. Some of the original 17th-century shingles can still be seen. The original fireplace with rounded corners and 17th-century oven, is remarkable. The garden, sloping down to the Town Brook, will delight the visitor.

HOWLAND HOUSE   The Jabez Howland House, 33 Sandwich Street, is the only house now standing in Plymouth where Pilgrims are known to have lived. It was built in 1666 by Jacob Mitchel and acquired in 1667 by Jabez Howland, son of the Pilgrim John and Elizabeth (Tilley) Howland. "Owned and occupied by Jabez Howland before the death of his father and mother, it is fair to presume that its floors have been trodden by those two passengers of the MAYFLOWER, and that its walls have listened to their voices," says William T. Davis. The house was purchased by the Pilgrim John Howland Society in 1912 and restored in 1914.

The original house consisted of the two rooms to the right of the door. The left side was added in 1750, with the rear rooms at later dates. The furnishings are appropriate to the two periods.

HARLOW
OLD
FORT
HOUSE
1677

This old house was built by Sergeant William Harlow from timber granted him when the Fort on Burial Hill was dismantled. Here the household arts of the women of Plymouth Colony — spinning, weaving, candlemaking, etc.—are explained and demonstrated. The house is half a mile south of the Post Office. It is owned and maintained by the Plymouth Antiquarian Society.

SPOONER
HOUSE
1749

The Spooner House, 27 North Street, near Coles Hill and Plymouth Rock, was the home of the Spooner family from 1763 until the death of James Spooner, its last private owner, 1954. He left the house for use as a museum. It is maintained by the Plymouth Antiquarian Society.

In its pleasant interior may be seen the treasures of all the generations of Spooners that have lived here, — fine old furniture, mirrors, family portraits, china, etc.

The family might well return tomorrow. It is "a museum you could live in."

MAYFLOWER SOCIETY HOUSE 1754

This fine old house, situated where Winslow Street joins North Street, is the national headquarters of the General Society of Mayflower Descendants. It was built in 1754 by Edward Winslow, great-grandson of Edward Winslow, the Pilgrim. The front rooms of the house still contain their fine original panelling.

The Winslows were Royalists, and left Plymouth for Nova Scotia at the time of the Revolution. The house came into the Jackson family, and here Lydian Jackson was married to Ralph Waldo Emerson in 1835. In 1941 it was purchased by the General Society of Mayflower Descendants, who here hold their Triennial Conventions.

The house is open to the public during the summer months.

ANTIQUARIAN HOUSE
1809

"A Museum you could live in." Built 1809; purchased 1830 by Thomas Hedge, a Plymouth merchant whose family occupied it for nearly a hundred years. It is distinguished by its delicate proportions and interesting octagonal rooms. Its furniture and household appointments are unusually complete. The dolls and toys in its nursery, the Lowestoft, Canton, and Staffordshire wares in its china closets, and its collection of 19th-century costume, are all outstanding.

The Antiquarian House is on Water Street, facing the Town Wharf. It is owned and maintained by the Plymouth Antiquarian Society.

TOWN RECORDS
TOWN OFFICES
MEMORIAL HALL
The Records of the Town of Plymouth, as distinct from those of Plymouth Colony, begin in 1636. They are in the custody of the Town. The earliest, 1636-1783, have been published, and may be consulted at the Public Library or at Pilgrim Hall. THE TOWN OFFICES are on Lincoln Street; the building was erected in 1891 as a High School, and re-fitted for its present use in 1953. MEMORIAL HALL, on Court Street at Memorial Drive, was dedicated in 1926 to all Plymouth citizens serving their country under arms since 1620. It contains a large auditorium, seating nearly 2000, a smaller hall seating 400, and rooms for various patriotic organizations.

COURT HOUSE
REGISTRY OF
DEEDS AND PROBATE
The Plymouth County Court House, on Court Street, was built in 1820. It has been remodeled and enlarged at various times. It was in this building, then not quite completed, that a banquet was held, following Daniel Webster's famous oration on the 200th Anniversary of The Landing of the Pilgrims. The first celebration of The Landing was conducted by the Old Colony Club in 1769.

Near the Court House is the REGISTRY OF DEEDS AND PROBATE, a fireproof building erected in 1904. The records extend from current entries to the original Records of Plymouth Colony, eighteen manuscript volumes, dated 1633-1691, in the handwriting of Bradford, Winslow, and other officers of the Colony. They cover the Proceedings of the General Court and the Court of Assistants; Deeds and Indian Records; Wills and Inventories; Judicial Acts; Laws; Treasurers' Accounts; Births, Marriages and Deaths; and Miscellaneous Records. Here also is Plymouth Colony's copy of the Proceedings of the United Colonies of New England, a seventeenth-century experiment in handling common problems somewhat akin to the United Nations of today. Here, too, is the Patent of 1629/30 made out to William Bradford and Associates by the Earl of Warwick for the Council for New England, and transferred by

Bradford to the "whole body of Freemen" of the colony. With it is the curious little box in which it was sent over from England.

THE PLYMOUTH PUBLIC LIBRARY is on North Street. It had its beginnings in 1856 as a private organization, but the Town also contributes to its support, its contribution in 1962 being $55575.00. The main building was erected in 1902; the "Lindens" annex opened in 1960. The reading room and historical and genealogical books are available to visitors as well as to Plymouth residents.

THE OLD COLONY MEMORIAL, Plymouth's weekly newspaper, has been published continuously since May 4, 1822.

THE TOWN WHARF is the berth of Plymouth's picturesque fishing fleet; fishing and party-boats are also based there.

THE STATE PIER, where MAYFLOWER II is berthed from mid-April through Thanksgiving Day, is the official landing-place for out-of-town craft.

THE PLYMOUTH YACHT CLUB has its pier beyond Town Brook. Between them lies a convenient YACHT BASIN, and an excellent boat yard and marine railway. In summer the anchorage is gay with boats of all kinds. Probably more craft tie up in the Yacht Basin than frequented Plymouth in the days of its busiest marine prosperity, when the Grand Banks fishery, the West India and coastwise trades, and even occasional voyages to more distant ports were an important part of the business of the town. Then "the Waterside" bristled with wharves. In time they became obsolete. They were removed at the time of the Tercentenary Celebration of the Landing of the Pilgrims; the present State Park occupies their site.

TOURIST INFORMATION
PLYMOUTH INFORMATION CENTER
PLYMOUTH AREA CHAMBER
OF COMMERCE

An Information Center is maintained by the Town of Plymouth and the Plymouth Area Chamber of Commerce, as headquarters for information helpful to the visitor. It is on Park Avenue, Routes 44 and 3A. Leave Route 3 at exit to Route 44.

Plymouth offers the vacationing family an opportunity for family fun with sixteen parks, eight playgrounds, five bathing beaches, four picnic areas, two camp grounds, two municipal trailer parks, and three miles of seashore beach. An 18-hole golf course is open all the year round for golf enthusiasts. Fishing and party-boats ply in Plymouth harbor. Many clear fresh-water lakes, some stocked with game fish, invite the bather or angler.

For advance information, write Plymouth Area Chamber of Commerce. When in Plymouth, consult the Information Center. Make your reservations there for accommodations during your visit to Plymouth.

CHURCHES

Bethel AME Church, 6 Sever Street
Chiltonville Congregational Church, River Street
Christ Episcopal Church, Court and Lothrop Streets
Church of the Pilgrimage (Congregational), Town Square
Congregation Beth Jacob, 2 Pleasant Street
First Baptist Church, Summer Street and Westerly Road
First Church of Christ, Scientist, 190 Court Street
First Parish, Plymouth (Unitarian Universalist), Town Square
Memorial Methodist Church, Court and Brewster Streets
Nazarene Chapel, 6 Sever Street
North Methodist Church, 131 Standish Avenue
Reorganized Church of Jesus Christ of Latter Day Saints
Salvation Army, Carver Street
Second Church of Plymouth (Congregational), Manomet
St. Peter's Church, 81 Court Street
St. Mary's Church, 313 Court Street
St. Bonaventure's Church, Manomet

SERVICE ORGANIZATION MEETINGS

Kiwanis International — Ernie's Restaurant, Monday 6:30
Lions International — " " Thursday 6:45
Rotary International — Gov. Carver Motel, Monday 12:15

COMBINATION TICKETS, offering admission to the following museums at budget prices, may be purchased at the Information Center, or at any of the museums listed.

Antiquarian House	Mayflower II (ship)
Harlow Old Fort House	Pilgrim Hall Museum
Howland House	Plimoth Plantation
Mayflower Society House	Sparrow House
	Spooner House

THE COVER DESIGN, perhaps the earliest attempt to picture the Landing of the Pilgrims, is from an early 19th-century painting on glass. It belonged to John Watson, President of the Pilgrim Society in 1821; it now belongs to his descendant, Mrs. Robert B. Bowler.

THE PHOTOGRAPHS are from the files of the Pilgrim Society, Plimoth Plantation, the Plymouth Antiquarian Society, the Plymouth Area Chamber of Commerce, The Dicksons, Richard Vennerbeck, Randall Abbott, and the Christian Science Monitor.

Notes